Where We Live

Rural Homes

Heinemann
LIBRARY
Chicago, Illinois

T0052507

© 2014 Heinemann Library
an imprint of Capstone Global Library, LLC
Chicago, Illinois

To contact Capstone Global Library please phone 800-747-4992, or visit our website www.capstonepub.com

All rights reserved. No part of this publication may be reproduced or transmitted in any form or by any means, electronic or mechanical, including photocopying, recording, taping, or any information storage and retrieval system, without permission in writing from the publisher.

Edited by Daniel Nunn and Abby Colich
Designed by Cynthia Akiyoshi
Picture research by Mica Brancic
Production by Sophia Argyris
Originated by Capstone Global Library

Library of Congress Cataloging-in-Publication Data
Smith, Sian.
Rural homes / Sian Smith.—1st Edition.
pages cm.—(Where we live)
Includes bibliographical references and index.
ISBN 978-1-4329-8066-5 (hbk.)—ISBN 978-1-4329-8071-9 (pbk.) 1. Housing, Rural. I. Title.
HD7289.A3S65 2013
307.72—dc23 2012046423

Acknowledgments
We would like to thank the following for permission to reproduce photographs: Getty Images pp. 4 (National Geographic/Joy Tessman); 6, 23 bottom (Flickr/Ulrike Maier); 7, 23 centre bottom (AWL Images/Peter Adams); 9 (Robert Harding World Imagery/Eurasia); 12, 23 top (AFP Photo/Sabah Arar); 14 (AFP Photo/Rizwan Tabassum); 15 (Lonely Planet Images/Aldo Pavan); 16, 22 bottom right (Oxford Scientific/Trevor Worden); 18, 22 bottom left (Robert Harding World Imagery/Dallas & John Heaton); 19 (Photographer's Choice RF/Cristian Baitg); 20, 22 top right (Digital Vision/John Clutterbuck); 21, 23 centre top (Lonely Planet Images/Mark Daffey); Shutterstock pp. 5 (© Rob Marmion); 8 (© Radu Razvan); 10 (© S Reynolds); 11 (© Chrislofoto); 13, 22 top left (© iPics); SuperStock p. 17 (hemi/Hemis.fr/Franck Guiziou).

Front cover photograph of huts of the Tairona Indians, Colombia, reproduced with permission of Shutterstock (© urosr). Back cover photograph of a log cabin in Lapland, Finland reproduced with permission of Shutterstock (© iPics).

Every effort has been made to contact copyright holders of material reproduced in this book. Any omissions will be rectified in subsequent printings if notice is given to the publisher.

Printed in the United States 5483

Contents

Why Do People Need Homes? . . . 4
What Does Rural Mean? 6
Rural Homes. 8
What Are Rural Homes Made Of? 12
Unusual Rural Homes 16
Neighbors 20
Around the World 22
Picture Glossary. 23
Index 24

Why Do People Need Homes?

People live in homes.

Homes keep people safe.

What Does Rural Mean?

When something is rural, it is in the countryside. Villages are in rural places.

Rural places are far away from cities and large towns.

Rural Homes

There is more space to keep animals and grow plants in rural places.

Some people live on farms.

Some people live on ranches.

Some rural homes are large and have big yards.

What Are Rural Homes Made Of?

People sometimes use the materials around them to build rural homes.

Many homes are made of wood.

Some homes are made of mud or clay.

Some homes are made of stone or brick.

Unusual Rural Homes

Some homes are on stilts.

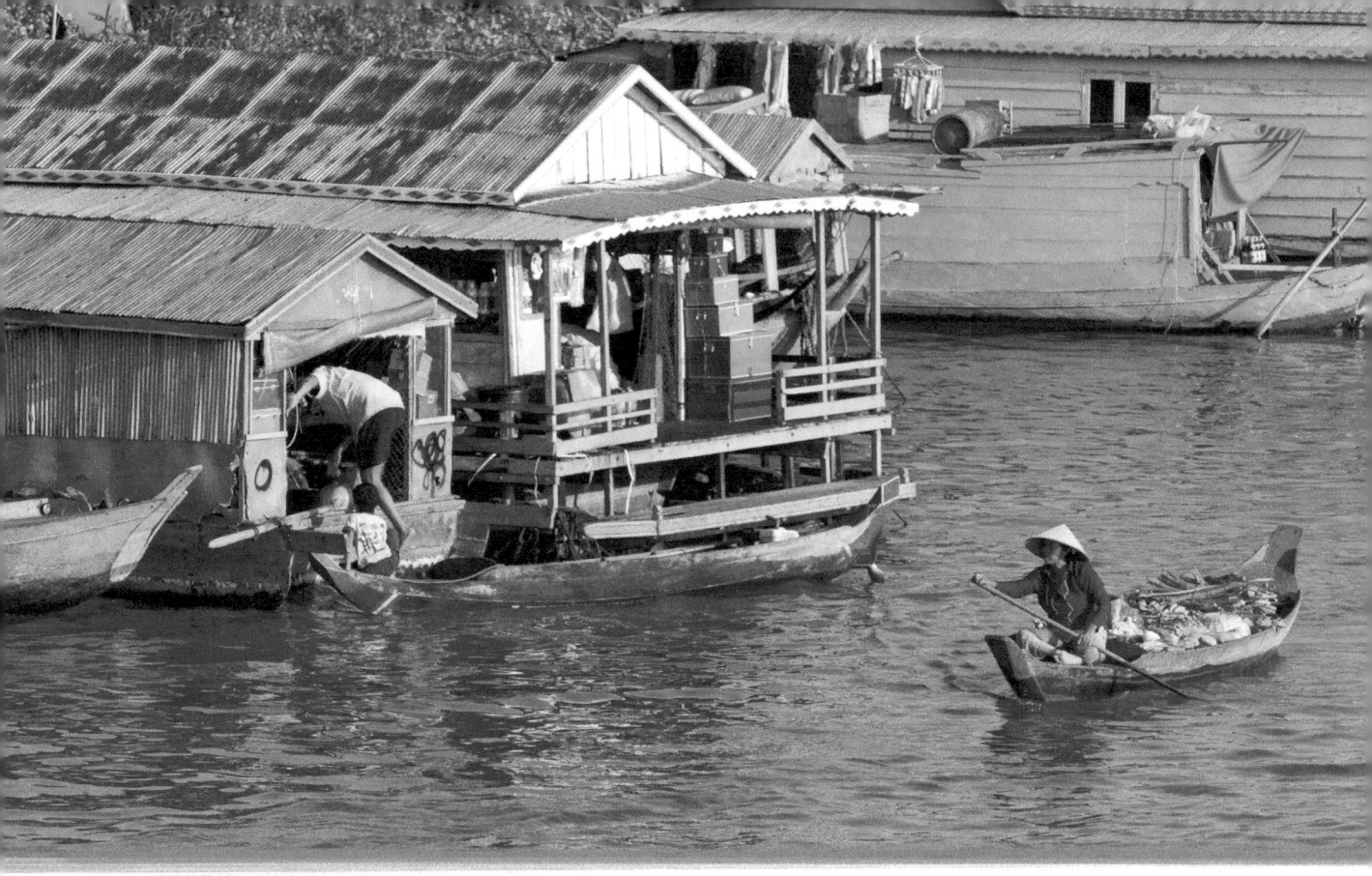

Some homes float on water.

Some homes are under the ground.

Some homes are in caves.

Neighbors

Some people in rural homes live far away from their neighbors.

Some people in rural homes live close to their neighbors.

Around the World

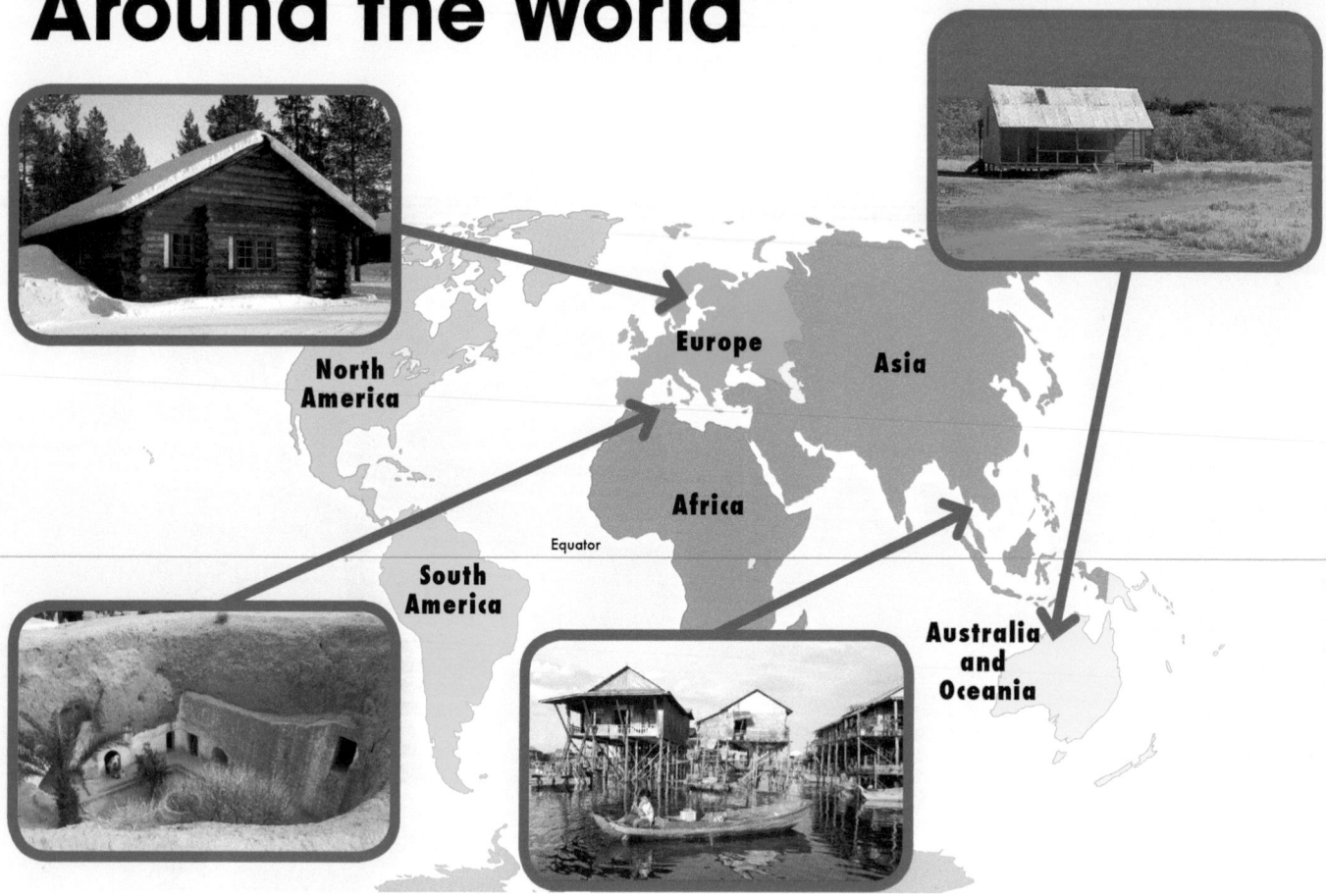

Follow the arrows to find out where each of these homes are found.

More information on page 24

Picture Glossary

material what something is made from. Wood and stone are types of material.

neighbors people who live near to you

rural countryside or places far away from cities

village place where people live in the countryside. A village is smaller than a town.

Index

countryside 6
caves 19
farms 9
neighbors 20, 21
ranches 10
stilts 16
villages 6
yards 11

Photograph information

The photographs in this book were taken from the following locations: p. 4 Namibia, Africa; p. 5 Viñales, Cuba; p. 6 Longsheng province, China; p. 7 Ethiopia, Africa; p. 8 the Alps, Switzerland; p. 9 Gwynedd, Wales; p. 11 England; p. 12 Najaf, Iraq; p. 13 Lapland, Finland; p. 14 Hyderabad, Pakistan; p. 15 Dang village, China; p. 16 floating village on Tonle Sap, Cambodia; p. 17 Chong Khneas floating village, Cambodia; p. 18 Matmata, Tunisia; p. 19 Uchisar Capadoccia, Turkey; p. 20 Broome, Australia; p. 21 Amantani Island, Peru.

Notes for parents and teachers

Introduce the children to the word *rural*. Explain that rural places are in the countryside where there's lots of space and fewer buildings (unlike cities and towns) and that there are rural places all over the world. Read the book together and ask the children what they think it might be like to live in the different types of rural homes. Discuss the materials the homes are made from and any special features. For example, homes made from mud or clay and homes that are under the ground tend to stay cool in hot weather. Look at the pictures on pages 20 and 21 together. Why do the children think it would be important to have good neighbors when you live in a rural place? Encourage the children to draw a picture of their favorite type of rural home and to write a sentence describing it.